PERPLEXING
LATERAL
THINKING
PUZZLES

&

Paul Sloane & Des MacHale

Illustrated by Myron Miller

SCHOLASTIC INC.
New York Toronto London Auckland Sydney
Mexico City New Delhi Hong Kong

ISBN 0-439-07743-5

Published by Scholastic Inc., 555 Broadway, New York, NY 10012,
by arrangement with Sterling Publishing Company, Inc.
SCHOLASTIC and associated logos are trademarks and/or registered
trademarks of Scholastic Inc.

12 11 10 9 8 7 6 5 4   9/9 0 1 2 3 4/0

Printed in the U.S.A.   40

First Scholastic printing, February 1999

Edited by Claire Bazinet

Acknowledgments

We would like to acknowledge the input and inspiration of many people, including those too numerous to mention by name from all over the world, who have written to us with ideas and encouragement. Also to the contributors to the *rec.puzzles* newsgroup on Internet who have given comments and feedback on some early ideas for this book.

This book could not have been produced without the help in editing and reviewing provided by Ann, Jackie and Val Sloane.

CONTENTS

· ·

· ·

Three men rode into town on Monday. One of them was the father of another one's son. All three wore colored hats but none of them knew the color of his own hat. One always spoke the truth, one always lied and the one who did not have a red hat alternated between lies and truth.

They walked into a bar and each put $10 on the bar top. The barman was a perfect logician who lived on the 16th floor of an apartment block but never took the elevator down. He gave each man $1 change and kept $2 for himself.

The first man asked for a glass of water, whereupon the barman pulled a gun and shot him. The man said "Thank you" and died, accidentally knocking over a goldfish bowl as he fell.

The second man put down twelve balls, one of which was different, and asked for a whiskey on the rocks. He took one sip and gasped, "This tastes of albatross!" before shooting himself.

The third man was a one-armed surgeon who carried an alligator under his arm. He stood on a block of ice and asked the barman, "Do you serve midgets?" The barman replied "Yes, we do." "OK then, make it a large brandy for me and a midget for the alligator!"

Who was the liar?

—Paul Sloane, posting to
rec.puzzles newsgroup, 1995

INTRODUCTION

If you have seen these kinds of puzzle before, you will know that they consist of strange situations which require an explanation. They are designed as a form of game for a small group, where one person knows the answer and the others try to figure it out by asking questions. The questions can only be answered by yes, no or irrelevant. The puzzles in this way can also be used as a form of training because they test and encourage skills in questioning, imagination, inductive reasoning and lateral thinking.

Sure, some of the situations are implausible. And sure, it is possible to come up with alternative solutions that fit the original puzzle. In fact, you can play a variation of the game where people try to think of as many alternative explanations as possible. But in general, you will get the most enjoyment from these puzzles if you keep questioning until you come up with the answer given in the book. There is a clues section to help out when you get stuck, but the best resource is always your own imagination.

THE PUZZLES

Aquamarine

The Late Report

A man and his wife went on vacation. Two months later, the man called the police to report the location of a body near the place where he had been on holiday. The police thanked the man and then asked why it had taken him two months to report the body. What was the reason?

Clues: 58/Answer: 80.

The Stranger in the Bar

Two men went out for a drink together in a bar. One of them looked up, saw a tall, dark stranger looking like death and drinking soda water, and pointed him out to his companion. Startled and uneasy, the two men left and went to another bar some miles away. After a few minutes, they looked up and saw the same sad, pale stranger drinking soda water. Deciding to leave, they went to a third bar, which was empty except for a young couple. However, within a few minutes, the cadaverous man appeared and, in a slow, sad voice, ordered a soda water. Almost out of his mind, one of the men went over to him and said, "Who are you and what do you want?" What did the man answer?

Clues: 65/Answer: 86.

Gertrude

When Gertrude entered the plane she caused her own death and the deaths of 200 people. Yet she was never blamed or criticized for her actions. What happened?

Clues: 55/Answer: 78.

Mad Cow Ideas

In 1996, the British government was faced with the task of slaughtering many thousands of healthy cattle in order to allay fears over the disease BSE, or mad cow disease. What proposal did the government of Cambodia make to help solve the problem?

Clues: 60/Answer: 81.

11

February 1866

What happened in February 1866 that will not happen again for another two and a half million years?

Clues: 53/Answer: 76.

The Cabbie's Revenge

An American tourist in London took a taxi cab. When he reached his destination, the tourist paid the taxi driver the fare, but did not include a tip. The taxi driver was displeased and said something to the American that ruined his whole evening. The two men were strangers and had never met previously. What did the cabbie say?

Clues: 50/Answer: 73.

Where in the World?

In what place would you find Julius Caesar, the biblical Rachel, King David, Pallas Athena (the Goddess of War), King Charlemagne, Alexander the Great, Queen Elizabeth I of England and Sir Lancelot all together?

Clues: 69/Answer: 90.

Scout's Honor

A boy scout was anxious to win maximum points at his monthly inspection. However, despite his mother's best efforts, she could not remove some blue felt-tip marker stains from his hands. What did she do?

Clues: 63/Answer: 84.

The King's Favor

When King Charles II of England visited a College at the University of Cambridge, he noticed a fine portrait of his father, King Charles I, hanging in the Main Hall. He asked if he could have it, but the ruling body of the College was very reluctant to part with it. At last the King said that he would grant the College anything in his power if they would give him the portrait and that he would be very displeased and unhelpful if they declined this generous offer. The College elders accepted. What did they ask for in return?

Clues: 58/Answer: 80.

Price Tag
....

Many shops have prices set just under a round figure, e.g., $9.99 instead of $10 or $99.95 instead of $100. It is assumed that this is done because the price seems lower to the consumer. But this is not the reason the practice started. What was the original reason for this pricing method?

Clues: 63/Answer: 84.

Color-Blind
....

John was color-blind. Because of this affliction, he landed an important job. What was it?

Clues: 51/Answer: 74.

Seaside Idea
....

A military commander during World War II was on leave so he took his children to the seaside for a day. Here, he got the idea he needed in order to successfully carry out his next assignment. What was the idea?

Clues: 63/Answer: 85.

The Hammer
....

Adam was jealous of Brenda's use of a computer. He changed that by means of a hammer. After that, he could use the computer, but Brenda could not. What did he do?

Clues: 57/Answer: 79.

The Stranger in the Hotel

A woman was sitting in her hotel room when there was a knock at the door. She opened the door to see a man whom she had never seen before. He said, "Oh I'm sorry. I have made a mistake. I thought this was my room." He then went off down the corridor to the elevator. The woman went back into her room and phoned reception to ask them to apprehend the man, who she was sure was a thief. What made her so sure?

Clues: 65/Answer: 86.

Buttons

There is a reason why men's clothes have buttons on the right while women's have buttons on the left. What is it?

Clues: 49/Answer: 73.

Upstairs, Downstairs

In a very exclusive restaurant several dozen diners are eating a top-class meal upstairs. Downstairs, precisely the same meal is being served at the same number of empty places where there is nobody to eat it. What is going on?

Clue: 68/Answer: 89.

Souper

A woman was at an expensive and prestigious dinner. The first course was soup. Halfway through the course, she called over a waiter and whispered in his ear. He brought a drinking straw which she used to finish her soup. The other guests were surprised at her actions, but she had a good explanation. What was it?

Clues: 65/Answer: 86.

Early Morning in Las Vegas

A gambler went to Las Vegas. He won on the roulette table, lost at blackjack and won at poker. When he went to bed in his hotel room, he carefully double-locked his door. At 3 a.m. he was awakened by the sound of someone banging and rattling on the door of his room. What did the person want and what did the gambler do?

Clues: 52/Answer: 75.

Inspired Composition

A composer of music sat looking out of a window, hoping for inspiration. Suddenly something he saw provided him with the opening theme for a new work. What did he see?

Clues: 57/Answer: 79.

Large Number

Assume there are approximately 5,000,000,000 (5 billion) people on earth. What would you estimate to be the result, if you multiply together the number of fingers on every person's left hands? (For the purposes of this exercise, thumbs count as fingers, for five fingers per hand.) If you cannot estimate the number, then try to guess how long the number would be.

Clues: 58/Answer: 80.

Inner Ear

An insect flying into a girl's ear terrifies her. Her mother rushes the girl to the doctor, but he is unable to remove the insect. Suddenly, the mother has an idea. What is it?

Clue: 57/Answer: 79.

The Single Flower

A woman was shown into a large room which contained over a thousand flowers. She was told that all but one of the flowers were artificial. She had to identify the real flower, but she could not examine the flowers closely nor smell them. She was alone in the room. What did she do to identify the single flower?

Clues: 64/Answer: 85.

Unseen

As far as it is possible to ascertain, there is one thing which only one man in recorded history has not seen. All other men who have sight have seen it. The man was not blind and lived to a ripe old age. What was it that he never saw and how come?

Clues: 67/Answer: 88.

The Champion's Blind Spot

At the dinner to celebrate the end of the Wimbledon tennis championship, the men's singles winner turned to the man next to him and said, "There is something here which you can see and all the other men can see but which I cannot see." What was it?

Clues: 50/Answer: 73.

The Task

Several people are waiting to perform a task which they usually do by themselves very easily. Now, however, they are all in need of the services of someone who usually performs the task only with difficulty. What is going on?

Clues: 66/Answer: 87.

WALLY Test I

From the World Association for Learning, Laughter and Youth (WALLY) comes another quickfire WALLY test. It consists of mean questions designed to trip you up. Test your wits now by writing down the answers to these questions. You have two minutes to complete the test.

1. There were eight ears of corn in a hollow stump. A squirrel can carry out three ears a day. How many days does it take the squirrel to take all the ears of corn from the stump?
2. Which triangle is larger—one with sides measuring 200, 300 and 400 cm or one with sides measuring 300, 400 and 700 cm?
3. How far can a dog run into a wood?
4. Which of the following animals would see best in total darkness: an owl, a leopard or an eagle?
5. What was the highest mountain in the world before Mount Everest was discovered?
6. Where are the Kings and Queens of England crowned?
7. If the Vice-President of the USA were killed, who would then become President?
8. Which candles burn longer—beeswax or tallow?
9. A farmer had 4 haystacks in one field and twice as many in each of his other two fields. He put the haystacks from all three fields together. How many haystacks did he now have?
10. What five-letter word becomes shorter when you add two letters to it?
11. Which weighs more—a pound of feathers or a pound of gold?
12. What has four legs and only one foot?

See solution to this WALLY Test on page 91.

Orange

What a Jump!

A man jumped 150 feet entirely under his own power. He landed safely. How did he do it?

Clues: 68/Answer: 89.

The String and the Cloth

A man lay dead in a field next to a piece of string and a cloth. How did he die?

Clues: 65/Answer: 86.

A Riddle

Four men sat down to play.
They played all night till break of day.
They played for gold and not for fun,
With separate scores for everyone.
When they came to square accounts
They all made quite fair amounts.
Can you this paradox explain?
If no one lost, how could all gain?

Clues: 63/Answer: 84.

Bad Impression

A man entered a city art gallery and did terrible damage to some very valuable Impressionist paintings. Later that day, instead of being arrested, he was thanked by the curator of the art gallery for his actions. How come?

Clues: 48/Answer: 72.

The Animal

At the Carlton Club, Alan Quartermaine was telling one of his stories. "When the animal emerged from the lake I could see that its four knees were wet," he said. Marmaduke, who had walked into the room at that very point, then interrupted, "I know what kind of an animal that was." How did he know and what kind of animal was it?

Clues: 48/Answer: 72.

Escape

A man was trapped on an island in the middle of a large and deep lake. He could not swim and had no boat or means of making one. He waited desperately for help, but none came. Eventually he managed to escape. How?

Clues: 52/Answer: 75.

Poisoned

A man is found dead in a locked room. He has died of poisoning and it looks like suicide. No one was with him when he took the poison. But it was, in fact, murder. How come?

Clues: 62/Answer: 84.

Failed Forgery

A master forger forged a US $100 bill. The bills he made were perfect copies of the original in every detail, yet he was caught. How?

Clues: 52/Answer: 75.

Apprehended

Some time ago a burglar ransacked a house in the middle of the night and left without anybody seeing him. Yet the police picked him up within a few hours. How did they trace him?

Clues: 48/Answer: 72.

The Metal Ball
....

At the beginning of his act, a magician places a solid metal ball, 4 inches in diameter, on a table and places a cover over it. At the end of his act when he lifts the cover, the ball has disappeared. How?

Clues: 60/Answer: 82.

One Croaked!
....

Two frogs fell into a large cylindrical tank of liquid and both fell to the bottom. The walls were sheer and slippery. One frog died but one survived. How?

Clues: 61/Answer: 83.

Unspoken Understanding

A deaf-and-dumb man went into a subway. He walked up to the cashier's booth and gave the cashier a dollar. The subway tokens cost 40 cents each. The cashier gave the man two tokens. Not a word was said, nor any sign given. How did the cashier know that the man indeed wanted two tokens?

Clues: 68/Answer: 89.

His Widow's Sister

It was reported in the paper that Jim Jones had married his widow's sister. How did he do this?

Clues: 57/Answer: 79.

Light Years Ahead

If you could travel faster than the speed of light, then you could catch up with the light which radiated from your body some time ago. You would then be able to see yourself as you used to be when you were younger. Although faster-than-light travel is impossible, at least at this time, how can we catch up with the light that we radiated earlier and see ourselves directly—as we used to be? (Such captured images as photographs, movies and videotape do not count.)

Clues: 59/Answer: 80–81.

The Newspaper

Jim and Joe were fighting, so their mother punished them by making them both stand on the same sheet of yesterday's newspaper until they were ready to make up. She did this in such a way that neither of the boys could touch the other. How did she manage to do this?

Clues: 61/Answer: 82.

Light Work

There are 3 light switches outside a room. They are connected to three light bulbs inside the room. Each switch can be in the on position or the off position. You are allowed to set the switches and then to enter the room once. You then have to determine which switch is connected to which bulb. How do you do it?

Clues: 58/Answer: 80.

What a Bore!

An office worker has a colleague in her office outstaying his welcome. She can see that he is not inclined to leave any time soon. Concerned about his feelings, how does she manage to get rid of him without offending him?

Clues: 68/Answer: 89.

Soviet Pictures

During the dark days of the Soviet Union, purges took place following which experts in photography would doctor photographs to remove individuals who had been purged. How was one expert caught out?

Clues: 65/Answer: 86.

Penniless

A struggling author receives a present of $2000 from a lady admirer. He does not tell his wife about this cash gift, although she has shared all his trials and is very supportive. How did she find out that he had received the money?

Clues: 62/Answer: 83.

The Deadly Suitcase

A woman opened a suitcase and found to her horror that there was a body inside. How had it got there?

Clues: 51/Answer: 74.

Unknown Character

A recluse who had lived for many years in a small community was charged with a serious crime. He knew nobody in the area. Whom did he call as a character witness?

Clues: 66/Answer: 87.

Gasoline Problem

A man's car runs out of gasoline. His car tank holds exactly 13 gallons. He has three empty unmarked containers which can hold 3 gallons, 6 gallons and 11 gallons. Using only these containers at the gas station, how can the man bring back exactly 13 gallons? He is not allowed to buy more than 13 gallons and dispose of the extra.

Clue: 55/Answer: 78.

Poison Pen

A woman received a very nasty, anonymous letter containing threats and allegations. She called the police and they quickly found out who had sent it. How?

Clues: 62/Answer: 84.

The Coconut Millionaire

A man buys coconuts at $5 a dozen and sells them at $3 a dozen. As a result of this he becomes a millionaire. How come?

Clues: 51/Answer: 74.

The Music Stopped Again

When the music stopped, he died very suddenly. How?

Clues: 61/Answer: 82.

Disreputable

A man was born before his father, killed his mother and married his sister. Yet he was considered normal by all those who knew him. How come?

Clues: 51/Answer: 75.

Personality Plus

An agency offered personality assessment on the basis of handwriting. How did an enterprising client show that the operation was unreliable?

Clue: 62/Answer: 83.

Gambler's Ruin

Syd Sharp, a first-class card player, regularly won large amounts at poker. He was also excellent at bridge, black-jack, cribbage, canasta, and pinochle. Joe, on the other hand, was terrible at cards; he could never remember what had gone before or figure out what card to play next. One day, Joe challenged Syd to a game of cards for money. Over the next couple of hours, Joe proceeded to win quite a large amount from Syd. How?

Clues: 55/Answer: 78.

WALLY Test II

Just when you thought you were safe—another WALLY test! Write down the answer to each question as soon as possible after reading it. You have two minutes to complete the test.

1. Which two whole numbers multiplied together make 17?
2. If post is spelled POST and most is spelled MOST, how do you spell the word for what you put in the toaster?
3. What word of five letters contains six when two letters are taken away?
4. A Muslim living in England cannot be buried on Church ground even if he converts to Christianity. Why not?
5. How many bananas can a grown man eat on an empty stomach?
6. Why is it that Beethoven never finished the Unfinished Symphony?
7. What common word is pronounced wrongly by over half of all Yale and Harvard graduates?
8. What gets larger the more you take away?
9. If I gave you ten cents for every quarter you could stand on edge and you stood three quarters on their edge, how much money would you gain?
10. If there are 12 six-cent stamps in a dozen, then how many two-cent stamps are there in a dozen?

See solution to this WALLY Test on page 92.

Yellow

Fast Work

When she was picked up, it was discovered that Marion had married ten men. They were all still alive but no charges were pressed against her. Why not?

Clues: 53/Answer: 76.

The Flicker

A man was running along a corridor clutching a piece of paper. He saw the lights flicker. He gave a cry of anguish and walked on dejectedly. Why?

Clues: 54/Answer: 77.

An American Shooting

One American man shot dead another American man in full view of many people. The two men had never met before and did not know each other. Neither was a policeman nor a criminal. The man who shot and killed the other man was not arrested or charged with any crime. Why not?

Clues: 48/Answer: 72.

King George

King George the Third of England suffered a temporary bout of madness. A movie was made in England on this subject. It was entitled "The Madness of George III," but this name was changed for American audiences. Why?

Clue: 58/Answer: 80.

Fallen Angel

A butterfly fell down and a man was seriously injured. Why?

Clues: 52–53/Answer: 76.

The Flaw in the Carpet

A man bought a very expensive oriental carpet in a reputable carpet shop in a Middle Eastern country. After he had bought it he found that it had a flaw. He took it back to the shop. It was agreed that there was a flaw in the carpet but the shopkeeper refused to take back the carpet or give any kind of refund or reduction in price. Why not?

Clues: 54/Answer: 77.

What a Relief!

Immediately after the end of World War II, a doctor in France approached a soldier who was perfectly healthy and asked for a large sample of his urine. Why was this?

Clues: 68–69/Answer: 89.

First Choice

A travel article on Brazil observed that, in restaurants in Rio, soup was a very popular starter choice for rich ladies. Why?

Clues: 54/Answer: 77.

Disturbance

A man went to his neighbor's house at 3 in the morning and started shouting and banging on the door. He would not stop until the neighbors opened the door and stood facing him. Initially angry, they later thanked the man. Why?

Clues: 52/Answer: 75.

Mona Lisa

Why did a group of enterprising thieves steal the famous painting the Mona Lisa and then return it undamaged a few months later?

Clues: 60/Answer: 82.

Snow Joy

Children in a town in New England were delighted one snowy January day. The snow was so heavy that school had to be canceled. Their joy continued when the deep snow caused the same thing to happen on the next few days. Then they became disappointed and upset at having to miss school. Why?

Clues: 64/Answer: 86.

The Cheat

A man cheated a woman out of a sum of $5. When she found out, she killed him. They were not poor. Her defense lawyer argued that she was justified in her actions, and many people agreed with him. Why?

Clues: 50/Answer: 74.

Dutch Race

One of the most prestigious races in Holland involves many people and enormous organization. But nobody knows when it will be held until two days before the race. Why?

Clue: 52/Answer: 75.

Wino

A man was enjoying his meal at a dinner party and had just started a delicious dessert. Why did he deliberately knock over the salt cellar into his dessert and ruin it?

Clues: 69/Answer: 90.

Garden Story

Why did a man tell his wife that he had buried guns in their garden when he knew that he had not?

Clues: 55/Answer: 78.

Fireworks Display

A young family went out to a fireworks display. On their return, the parents were very sad. Why?

Clues: 54/Answer: 77.

The Fallen Guide

A mountain climber in the Himalayas took along with him two mountain guides. After a few hours, one of the guides fell into a deep crevasse. The climber and the other guide continued the climb and did not raise the alarm. Why?

Clues: 53/Answer: 76.

The Yacht Incident
• •

A yacht is found floating in the middle of the ocean and around it in the water are a dozen human corpses. Why?

Clues: 69/Answer: 90.

Self-Addressed Envelope
• •

Why does a man send himself a letter every day but Saturday?

Clues: 64/Answer: 85.

Fingered
• •

Why did a political candidate always place his finger on the chest of any man when he was canvassing them in public?

Clues: 54/Answer: 76.

The Gross Grocery List
• •

A woman handed a man a grocery list, but when he handed it back to her she was extremely embarrassed. Why?

Clues: 56/Answer: 78.

Finger Break
• •

Why did a woman take a baseball bat and break her husband's fingers?

Clues: 53/Answer: 76.

Unpublished

An eminent firm of publishers had a manuscript for a novel. It was written by a very well known author and was sure to sell well. However, they chose not to publish it. Why?

Clues: 67/Answer: 87–88.

The Unwanted Gift

A nobleman was very displeased when he received an expensive gift from the King. Why?

Clues: 68/Answer: 89.

Benjamin Franklin

Benjamin Franklin was a well-educated man. Why did he deliberately spell Philadelphia wrongly?

Clues: 48/Answer: 72.

Middle Eastern Muddle

One of the most successful advertising agencies in the USA acquired a Middle Eastern account. Their first ad there made them a laughingstock. Why?

Clues: 60/Answer: 82.

The Wounded Soldier

A badly wounded but conscious soldier is brought into a field hospital during a battle. The surgeon takes a quick look at him and then says to the orderly, "Get this man out of here! He is a coward who has smeared himself with the blood of his comrades." Why did he say this?

Clues: 69/Answer: 90.

Ice Rinked

A man skating at an ice rink saw a woman slip and fall. Although she was a stranger to him, he wanted to find out if she was all right. He went over to her, but before he said anything she slapped him hard across the face. They had never met or communicated before. Why did she strike him?

Clues: 57/Answer: 79.

On Time

Why did a man who knew the time and had two accurate watches phone the speaking clock?

Clues: 61/Answer: 83.

Cat Food

A man who did not like cats bought some fresh salmon and cream for a cat. Why?

Clue: 50/Answer: 73.

Rich Man, Poor Man

A man making over $10 million a year drives a small car, lives in a modest house, and insists he can't afford luxuries. Why not?

Clues: 63/Answer: 84.

Sleeping on the Job

A man undressed to go to bed and hundreds of people lost their jobs. Why?

Clues: 64/Answer: 85.

Fine Art

An art collector went into the art dealer, Sotheby's. He asked to have two items valued. One was an old violin and the other an oil painting. The experts studied them for days before confirming their remarkable findings. The collector was told that the two items were an original Stradivarius and a previously unknown work by Vincent van Gogh. At first, the collector was thrilled but later he became very dejected. Why?

Clues: 53/Answer: 76.

Ford's Lunch

Before hiring anyone in a senior post, Henry Ford, the auto magnate, always took the candidate out to dinner. Why?

Clues: 54–55/Answer: 77.

The Hairdresser

A New York City hairdresser recently said that he would rather cut the hair of three Canadians than one New Yorker. Why?

Clues: 56/Answer: 78.

Not a Hair

Lyndsey, an elegant fashion model and actor, was caught out in the rain one day during a photography session. Without hat or umbrella, she dashed through the rain for shelter. The strange thing was that not one hair on the model's head got wet. Why not?

Clues: 61/Answer: 83.

The Plate of Mushrooms

A man enjoyed the taste of mushrooms but had a morbid fear of being poisoned by them, so he never ate them. Yet one day he ordered a large plate of assorted mushrooms to eat. Why?

Clue: 62/Answer: 83.

Order Delayed

One night, a man staying in a small Tokyo hotel ordered a drink on room service. It never came. Early in the morning, he was awakened by a loud knock on his door. Why?

Clues: 62/Answer: 83.

Silence Is Golden

A distinguished speaker once gave a very interesting talk to a packed and enthusiastic audience. However, after the talk finished there was no applause whatsoever. Why?

Clues: 64/Answer: 85.

Bluebeard's Treasure

The pirate Bluebeard buried his treasure on a desert island. Some time later he heard that one of his enemies had obtained a copy of the map which showed the exact location of the treasure. But Bluebeard was not worried. Why not?

Clues: 49/Answer: 72–73.

The King

A man is crowned King. Shortly afterwards, he is captured by enemy forces and chopped in two. Why?

Clue: 57/Answer: 80.

Lockout

Jefferson Jones was an art collector with a valuable collection in his apartment. It had one door and he fitted it with six locks. While he was away, a determined burglar who was skilled at picking locks tried to open the door, but although he could pick the locks he could not get in. Why not?

Clues: 59–60/Answer: 81.

Creepy Crawly

On a trip deep in the Amazonian jungle, the explorer Alan Quartermaine woke one morning. He could feel something inside his sleeping bag. It had a head and a tail and it moved when he moved. However, he was calm and unafraid. Why?

Clues: 51/Answer: 74.

The Unlucky Trip

A man hurried down an unlit road with a torch in his hand. He tripped and dropped the torch, which went out. No damage was done and no one was was hurt, but the incident was reported in newspapers around the world. Why?

Clues: 66/Answer: 87.

The Murderer

Brown told Smith that he had just committed a murder. The two men had never met before. Smith was a responsible citizen and he believed Brown but he did not report him to the police. Why not?

Clues: 60–61/Answer: 82.

Truckload

A fully loaded truck that weighs exactly 10 tons starts to cross a long bridge which at its center can carry a load of exactly 10 tons—no more. As he reaches the center the driver hears the bridge creak so he slows right down. Just then, a flock of starlings lands on the roof of the truck but the bridge does not break. Why not?

Clues: 66/Answer: 87.

Fruitless Search

A man was searching for blue-back frogs in an area where they were very common. He caught one. It started to rain and he became frantic. The rain grew stronger and the man left, disconsolate. Why?

Clues: 55/Answer: 77.

Checked

A man wrote out and signed a check from his own checkbook for $1,000. There was more than this in his account. Yet he was charged with fraud. Why?

Clues: 51/Answer: 74.

These Puzzles

You have certainly noticed that the puzzles in this book are divided into three color categories. This was done for a reason that by now should be more or less apparent to you. This puzzle also fits the mold. So, why have the puzzles been placed in their particular categories?

Clues: 66/Answer: 87.

THE CLUES

An American Shooting

Although an innocent man was killed, no crime was committed.

Both men were armed.

This took place in the 19th century.

The Animal

Marmaduke was able to deduce what the animal was from Alan Quartermaine's statement alone.

Only one animal has just four knees.

Apprehended

The burglar left no clues inside the house.

The incident took place in the middle of winter.

Bad Impression

He deliberately sprayed water over the paintings. This damaged them.

He was not unstable, deranged or malevolent. He acted out of good intentions.

Benjamin Franklin

Benjamin Franklin deliberately spelled Philadelphia wrongly as part of his job. He was not involved in teaching.

He was trying to make things more difficult for those who made his job difficult.

Bluebeard's Treasure

The map did show the exact location of the treasure and the enemy would be able to reach the island and excavate the spot.

Bluebeard buried treasure in a way which he believed optimized his chances of recovering it.

Buttons

This is not a fashion issue. It has to do with right- and left-handedness.

When buttons first came into use, it was the better-off who used them.

The Cabbie's Revenge

The cabbie did not insult the American. He did not make any personal or nationalistic comment.

The cabbie gave the American a piece of factual information which the American did not want to hear. (We cannot tell you exactly what the cabbie said because it might ruin an evening for you too!)

The location to which the American was driven by the cabbie is important.

Cat Food

He wanted the cat to do something for him.

The Champion's Blind Spot

The winner had perfect eyesight and could see as well as any other person there but, nonetheless, they could see something he could not see.

He could not see something relative to him which others could see relative to them.

If the winner had lost a game, then he could not make this claim.

The Cheat

The man had failed to keep a promise.

He had not used the $5 as agreed.

The woman found herself considerably worse off than she had expected.

Checked

His signature was perfect.

He intended to defraud. The check looked fine but it would not have proven valid.

The Coconut Millionaire

He lost money on every coconut he sold.

He did not make money by any related activity.

Color Blind

He was employed by the military.

He could see things other people found difficult to see.

Creepy Crawly

It was not dangerous.

It was not alive—nor had it ever been.

The Deadly Suitcase

The body was that of a child who had died accidentally through suffocation.

The woman was poor and had tried to save money.

Disreputable

This is really three puzzles in one.

He was born after his father was. He did not murder his mother. He did not commit incest.

Disturbance

He was trying to warn them.

They were not in danger but he thought they were.

Dutch Race

The race can only take place under certain conditions. These conditions occur infrequently.

Early Morning in Las Vegas

The person who banged on the door was not a hotel official, nor a police officer or other such authority.

The gambler was not in danger.

Escape

He did not attract or receive help in the form of a boat or a plane. He crossed the lake under his own power.

He was lucky to have found shelter.

Failed Forgery

The paper he used was perfect. The color, texture and watermark were perfect.

His copy was accurate in every way, yet the bills he made had an error that made them easily identifiable as forgeries.

Fallen Angel

The butterfly was not a live butterfly.

The man walked into trouble.

The model butterfly served as a warning.

The Fallen Guide

The first guide fell into the deep ravine and was lost from view. Both the climber and the second guide were fit and healthy. They had time to try to rescue the first guide but they did not bother.

The climber believed that the first guide was not important to him and could be replaced.

Fast Work

Marion had committed no crime.

She was single.

February 1866

It was clearly visible to man but not of man's doing.

February 1866 lacked something that other months have.

Fine Art

The art collector learned that his two very valuable works were worth far less than he had assumed.

There was no mistake. Sotheby's correctly identified the works.

Finger Break

She had good intentions.

He was in danger.

Fingered

He was vain.

He wanted maximum publicity.

Fireworks.Display

The family consisted of two parents, their four-year-old daughter and their two-month-old baby son.

The fireworks display went perfectly. There were no accidents or injuries. The children enjoyed it.

The parents learned something.

First Choice

This had nothing to do with taste, nutrition, diet or food.

There was a practical reason why rich ladies preferred soup in restaurants. It did not apply at home.

The Flaw in the Carpet

The shop explained that, although there was a flaw in the carpet, it was not the result of an error or mistake.

The carpet makers were devout Muslims.

The Flicker

He knew that someone had died.

The piece of paper could have saved a life.

Ford's Lunch

Henry Ford was giving the person a form of test, althoughthe candidate for the position did not realize it.

He watched carefully as the candidate consumed his soup.

Fruitless Search

Blue-back frogs are now extinct.

The man was very religious.

He wanted to get back to his boat.

Gambler's Ruin

They played cards, but Joe chose a game that suited him better than it suited Syd.

Syd had a handicap at this particular child's game.

Garden Story

The man had lied, but not with the intention of deceiving his wife.

He was worried that the hard work of gardening would be a strain for his wife, who lived alone and had no one to help her.

Gasoline Problem

No complex mathematical combinations are needed to solve this one.

Gertrude

Gertrude caused a mechanical failure in the plane.

It was a jet aircraft.

The Gross Grocery List

The grocery list contained nothing more than a list of regular and ordinary groceries.

The man to whom she handed the list was not a grocer.

She had set out that morning with two lists.

The Hairdresser

The New York hairdresser had nothing against New Yorkers and has no particular love of Canadians.

He charges everyone the same price for one haircut.

The Hammer

Adam did not use the hammer on the computer. The computer was undamaged.

Brenda had a disability.

His Widow's Sister

When Jim Jones died, his wife became a widow.

No bigamy is involved and no life after death.

He had married his widow's sister quite legitimately.

Ice Rinked

She misunderstood his intentions.

Although he did not say a word, he did try to communicate with her.

Inner Ear

The mother lures the insect out of her daughter's ear.

Inspired Composition

He saw something which made no sound but which suggested a tune.

He saw some creatures at rest.

The King

Twelve men had started out in the attempt to become king. The one who succeeded was one of the few to survive.

King George

It was decided that the title might mislead audiences.

The King's Favor

In a way, the King got what he wanted and the College got what it wanted.

The King took the portrait along with him when he left Cambridge.

No copy was made.

The Late Report

The man was not involved in any way in the death of the person whose body he had reported.

The man had not noticed the body earlier, but did later.

Large Number

The answer can be quickly and accurately deduced.

Think about the effect of actually multiplying the number of fingers on the left hands of all the people in the world, one after another.

The calculation might start $5 \times 5 \times 5 \times 5 \times 5 \times 5 \times 5 \times 5 \times 4 \times 5 \times 5 \times 5 \times 5 \times \ldots$ and so on.

Light Work

With just two bulbs and two switches, it would be easy.

Light bulbs give out light. What else do they do when they are switched on?

Light Years Ahead

There is a way in which we can see the light which we radiated and therefore an image of the way we were.

It is a common experience to view this image.

Lockout

Given enough time, the burglar could pick each lock in turn, i.e., he could change its state from locked to unlocked or vice-versa.

It took the burglar half an hour to pick a lock. After two days of picking the locks he gave up and went home.

Mad Cow Ideas

The Cambodian government suggested a way for Britain to get rid of the suspect cattle without risking that the cattle would eventually be eaten.

The suggestion involved the eventual death of the cattle in a way that would help solve a Cambodian problem.

The Metal Ball

The magician need not do anything to make the ball vanish.

He carefully makes and stores the ball before his act.

Middle Eastern Muddle

They produced an ad which was misunderstood.

Their ad had no words.

Mona Lisa

They did it for money.

No insurance payment was involved. The thieves did not receive any reward or payment from the police, museum, insurance company or any public body.

The Murderer

Brown committed the murder and told Smith in all seriousness and with full detail. Smith was the first person to hear this or know that Brown had committed the murder.

Smith had nothing to gain from the murder. He was not a criminal, simply an honest and socially responsible citizen.

The Music Stopped Again

This has nothing to do with tightrope walkers!

A game was taking place. It involved music.

The Newspaper

Jim and Joe were normal boys aged seven and eight.

They both stood on the same sheet of newspaper but, try as they might, they could not touch or even see each other without leaving the newspaper.

Not a Hair

Everyone else who was caught in the rain was soaked.

Lyndsey's head got wet.

On Time

He was not interested in the time.

He wanted to make an innocuous telephone call.

He was cheating.

One Croaked!

The frogs were physically identical. One managed to survive the ordeal because of the result of its actions.

The nature of the liquid is important.

Order Delayed

The drink he ordered is relevant.

It was a type of lemonade.

Penniless

The author did not know the identity of the lady admirer.

His wife was not jealous or concerned about the gift.

Personality Plus

The client submitted handwriting tests. He then simply showed that the assessments were incorrect.

The Plate of Mushrooms

Although he still believed that one or more of the mushrooms might be poisonous, he no longer feared that the mushrooms would kill him.

Poison Pen

They examined the letter very carefully.

The letter came from a pad of writing paper.

Poisoned

The man was trying to gain sympathy. He was deceived.

The man wrote a suicide note and then deliberately took an overdose.

He did not intend to die. He expected to be rescued.

Price Tag

A price set at 5 cents, or even 1 cent, under a round dollar amount means that a customer would be entitled to change from a bill.

Smart shopkeepers were trying to protect themselves from losses.

Rich Man, Poor Man

The man makes over $10 million a year at his work but he does not have a lot to spend.

He is not wealthy, nor does he have any major debts or expenses.

A Riddle

They played seriously and each did his best.

Each man came out ahead.

No one joined their group.

Scout's Honor

She sent him to the inspection with the marks still on his hands.

She ensured that the marks would not be seen.

Seaside Idea

He was a senior officer in the Royal Air Force.

He and his children threw stones into the sea.

Self-Addressed Envelope

He posts a letter so that he will receive a letter.

He wants to be sure of seeing the postman on every possible delivery.

Silence Is Golden

The audience was not physically restrained from applauding the speaker. They simply chose not to.

The audience was made up entirely of women.

The Single Flower

She got some help.

No other person was involved.

Sleeping on the Job

The man was a movie star.

The people who lost their jobs worked in the garment industry.

Snow Joy

Naturally, the children would much rather be at home, or out playing, than go to school.

There was nothing special going on at school to attract the children back.

There was a consequence of an extended school cancellation which they did not want.

Souper

She was perfectly capable of consuming the soup with a spoon. There was nothing wrong with the soup.

Something happened halfway through the course which caused her to want to use the straw.

Soviet Pictures

A fault was found in the photograph which proved it had been tampered with.

A fault was discovered by a Count.

The Stranger in the Bar

The two men were drinking beer while the stranger was drinking soda water.

The two men hadn't noticed the stranger outside the bars, but there was a connection between them and the stranger.

The Stranger in the Hotel

Hers was a single room.

There was nothing unusual about the man's appearance or bearing. The woman made a deduction based on what he said.

The String and the Cloth

He died an accidental death.

He had been holding the string.

It was a windy day.

The Task

The person who is performing the task has a disability.

Circumstances have changed so that the person's disability gives him an advantage over the others.

These Puzzles

Each puzzle belongs to one and only one section, based on a single characteristic of the words of the puzzle.

The categories could have been called A, O and Y—but that is not as colorful!

Each puzzle is a question.

The Unlucky Trip

The torch was important.

The man was a runner.

Truckload

It is true that, when the starlings alight on the truck, their weight adds to it.

Despite the birds landing on the truck, the total weight of truck and birds never exceeds 10 tons.

Unknown Character

He called someone who did not know him.

By calling this person he hoped to prove that he was not a bad character.

Unpublished

The publication of the novel would not cause offense or any legal actions.

The title of the novel was well known.

Unseen

It is known that this man led a secluded life.

Other men, even those blind from birth, would hear and touch this thing, but this man never heard or touched it.

Unspoken Understanding

The man did want two tokens, and the cashier was able to correctly deduce this.

Nothing was written or signaled.

The Unwanted Gift

The gift was costly to maintain.

The gift was of a rare color.

Upstairs, Downstairs

The restaurant is in an unusual location.

What a Bore!

The woman arranges an interruption, but no one else is involved.

She enjoys the advantages of modern technology.

What a Jump!

He was an athlete.

He did not use any extra source of power but did use special equipment.

This happens regularly in a certain sporting event.

What a Relief!

The soldier's urine contained something of use to the doctor.

The soldier was an American GI.

This was a common practice among many French doctors.

Where in the World?

Their images are found together in one common place.

They are found on something which is in common use and has been for many years.

They are used in a form of game.

Wino

He did not want to eat the dessert, but didn't want to appear rude.

He was hungry, normally enjoyed this dessert and had started it with gusto. It had tasted good and he felt fine.

The Wounded Soldier

The soldier was genuinely wounded and was not a coward. The doctor knew this.

The doctor lied, but had good intentions and wanted to help the soldier.

The Yacht Incident

They had been passengers aboard the yacht.

They died because of an accident. They drowned.

THE ANSWERS

An American Shooting

This happened during the American Civil War. The men were soldiers in the opposing armies.

The Animal

Marmaduke knew that the only animal with four knees is the elephant.

Apprehended

It was during winter and the place was covered in snow. As the burglar backed his car to leave, he hit a snowbank and his number plate left a perfect impression in the snow.

Bad Impression

He was a firefighter who, in the course of putting out a fire, sprayed the room and paintings with water. He had indeed damaged the paintings, but saved them and others from complete destruction.

Benjamin Franklin

Benjamin Franklin was at one time in charge of the U.S. Mint. Forgery of banknotes was a great problem. He deliberately misspelled Philadelphia on a banknote in order to enable the detection of forgeries. Unfortunately for him, the forgers simply copied his deliberate mistake.

Bluebeard's Treasure

Bluebeard buried his treasure at the spot shown on the map. He knew that a copy of the map might be made, so he dug a shaft 30 feet deep and buried three-quarters of his treasure there. He covered that and filled in the shaft to a depth of 10 feet, where he buried a quarter of his treasure—which he was prepared to sacrifice to protect the rest. He reckoned that no one who had found substantial treasure at 10 feet would dig a further 20 feet and that once word got out that his treasure had been taken no one else would look for it.

Buttons

Most people are right-handed and find it easier to fasten a button which is on the right through a hole which is on the left. This is why men's buttons are on the right. When buttons were first used it was the better-off who could afford clothes with buttons. Among this class the ladies were often dressed by maid-servants. The servant would face the lady and so it was easier for right-handed servants to fasten buttons which were on the lady's left.

The Cabbie's Revenge

The American was going to a performance of the famous Agatha Christie play *The Mousetrap*. The taxi dropped him outside the theater. The spiteful taxi-driver said "X did it," where X was the name of the murderer in the play. (We cannot state here X's name or we might ruin your future enjoyment of the play!)

Cat Food

The man was a television cable engineer who needed to thread a cable from the back of a house, under the floor, to the front. He released the cat with a string attached to it into a hole at the back of the house. The cat was lured by the smell of the cream and salmon to find its way under the floor to the front of the house. The string was used to pull the cable through.

The Champion's Blind Spot

Every other competitor could see someone who had beaten them.

The Cheat

For five weeks in a row, the woman gave the man a dollar to buy a lottery ticket on her behalf. Feeling that her chances were nil, he kept the money. Her numbers came up on the fifth week, scooping the $10 million jackpot. She told all her friends and neighbors that she had won.

Checked

He used ink which vanished after a few hours.

The Coconut Millionaire

The man is a philanthropist who bought great quantities of coconuts to sell to poor people at prices they could afford. He started out as a billionaire, but lost so much money in his good works that he became a millionaire!

Color-Blind

John was employed by the Air Force during wartime to detect camouflaged enemy positions from aerial photographs. Camouflage is designed to fool people with normal vision. People who are color-blind are much better at spotting differences in the texture and shading of landscape.

Creepy Crawly

It was a coin.

The Deadly Suitcase

The body was that of the woman's son. They were flying to the USA to start a new life, but she did not have enough money for two airfares. She put him in a suitcase with tiny airholes. She did not know that the luggage compartment would be depressurized.

Disreputable

He was born in the presence of his father. His mother died at the birth. He became a pastor and married his sister to her husband.

Disturbance

The man had seen a stranger climb into the house through a window. Fearing for their safety, he woke his neighbors up. The "intruder" was a new lodger, who had forgotten his key. The alert man was thanked for his concern.

Dutch Race

The race is the famous "eleven towns race," the largest natural ice race in the world. Usually between 12,000 and 15,000 people take part over a course on the frozen canals and lakes in Holland. However, it can only take place after a sustained period of very cold weather. The right circumstances occur around once every ten years. The authorities prepare (for example, by banning factories from discharging warm waste water into the canals) and then give only two or three days' notice of the start of the race.

Early Morning in Las Vegas

He had played poker in his room with friends until 2 a.m. They had all had plenty to drink and he had failed to notice that one of his friends had fallen asleep behind his sofa. Later, the man woke up and rattled the door as he tried to get out. The gambler let him out.

Escape

He walked over the frozen lake.

Failed Forgery

He had copied a forged bill which itself contained a flaw.

Fallen Angel

The butterfly was made of plastic and was put on a large plate-glass window to indicate the presence of the glass. After it fell off, a man walked into the window and was seriously injured.

The Fallen Guide

One of the guides was a book.

Fast Work

Marion had been picked up for a ride to the church. She was a member of the clergy and had married the men to their wives. (She was often heard to say that she enjoyed "Marion" people!)

February 1866

There was no full moon. January and March of that year each had two full moons—a most unusual occurrence.

Fine Art

The collector was told that the two items were an original Stradivarius and a previously unknown work by Vincent van Gogh. Unfortunately, Stradivarius could not paint very well and Vincent van Gogh made terrible violins!

Finger Break

He was holding a live electric cable. The electricity had paralyzed the muscles in his arm. Her action freed him.

Fingered

He did this in case a photograph was being taken of the incident. He reasoned that no newspaper editor would edit out the candidate from a picture but leave his finger in.

Fireworks Display

The parents discovered that their baby son was deaf. He reacted to the sight of fireworks but not to loud bangs of fireworks which were out of sight.

First Choice

There had been a spate of robberies at expensive restaurants. The robbers would burst in and take jewelry and money from the people in the restaurant. If you are eating soup then you can quietly drop rings or other jewelry into the soup before the robbers reach your table.

The Flaw in the Carpet

Every oriental carpet has a deliberate flaw in its design pattern. Islamic carpet makers believe that to make a perfect carpet would be to challenge Allah, who alone is perfect.

The Flicker

The man was carrying a stay of execution for a condemned man who was due to die in the electric chair. When he saw the lights flicker, he knew that he was too late.

Ford's Lunch

Henry Ford watched the potential employee eating soup. If he put salt in his soup before tasting it, then he would not employ him. Since the candidate could not know how salty the soup was without tasting it, Ford felt that this indicated a closed mind rather than someone who would investigate a situation before taking action.

Fruitless Search

The man was Noah. He knew that if he did not find a second blue-back frog they would become extinct in the flood. Unfortunately, this is what happened.

Gambler's Ruin

Syd Sharp was a first-class card player but he had a bad stutter. Knowing that Syd would be unable to respond fast enough to verbally announce the turning up of matching cards that the game's rules required, Joe challenged him to a game of Snap!

Garden Story

The man was in prison. He knew that all his mail was read. He received a letter from his wife asking, "When should I plant the potatoes?" He replied, "Do not plant any potatoes. I have hidden some guns in the garden." A little later his wife wrote back, "Some policemen came and dug up all the back garden but they did not find anything." He replied, "Now plant the potatoes."

Gasoline Problem

The man uses the meter at the gas pump to measure out exactly 13 gallons. He puts 11 gallons in the large container and 2 gallons into one of the others.

Gertrude

Gertrude, a goose, had been sucked into a jet engine.

The Gross Grocery List

The man was a priest who was rather deaf. He asked people in confession to write their sins down and put them through the grill of the confessional. When he handed her back her grocery list, the woman realized that she must have given her list of sins to the grocer.

The Hairdresser

He gets three times as much money!

The Hammer

Brenda was blind and she depended on her Braille manual when using the computer. Alan flattened the pages with a hammer.

His Widow's Sister

Jim Jones married Ella in 1820. She died in 1830. In 1840 he married Ella's sister, Mary. She became his widow when he died in 1850. So in 1820 he had married his widow's sister.

Ice Rinked

As he approached the woman, he made a sign to ask if she was OK. He put his thumb and first finger together to make an O. This sign is often used in countries such as the USA or UK to mean, "Are you all right?" Unfortunately, the woman came from an Eastern Mediterranean country (such as Greece) where this same sign is an obscene gesture.

Inner Ear

She put the girl in a darkened room and placed a bright light near her ear. The insect emerged.

Inspired Composition

He saw some blackbirds sitting on telegraph wires. Their positions indicated a melody line.

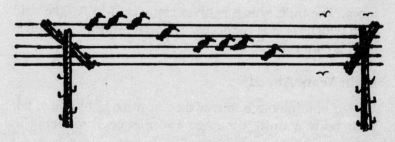

The King

This is normal in a game of checkers (or draughts).

King George

It was believed that many cinema-goers would mistakenly think it was the third in a series of movies, and would not go to see it because they had missed the first two. It was released as "The Madness of King George."

The King's Favor

The College asked the King to return the painting in six months. Since this was clearly in his power he agreed.

Large Number

The product of the number of fingers on the left hands of every person is zero. It only takes one person to have no fingers on their left hand for the product to be zero, because anything multiplied by zero is zero.

The Late Report

The man saw the body in the background on one of his holiday photographs. It was two months before the film was developed.

Light Work

You set switches A and B on and switch C off. You wait a few minutes and then switch B off. You then enter the room. The bulb which is on is connected to A. The cold bulb which is off is connected to C. The warm bulb which is off is connected to B.

Light Years Ahead

Yes—if you look in a mirror then you see light which left your body a finite time ago and has been reflected to reach your eyes. You see yourself as you were—not as you are!

Lockout

Jefferson Jones left three locks locked and three locks unlocked. He knew which was in which state, but the burglar did not. When the burglar eventually picked a lock which had been unlocked, he locked it. Try as he might, he could never get all six unlocked together.

Mad Cow Ideas

The Cambodian Government suggested that the cattle be sent to Cambodia and allowed to wander their fields to explode the many mines left over from their wars.

The Metal Ball

The disappearing ball was a ball of frozen mercury, which was taken from a freezer. It melted during the course of the act.

Middle Eastern Muddle

The agency forgot that people in the Middle East read from right to left. People saw a series of pictures showing the "before" and "after" for the use of washing powder. It indicated to them that the powder made clean clothes dirty.

Mona Lisa

The thieves handed the Mona Lisa back but not before they sold a dozen fake copies to gullible art collectors, each of whom believed he was buying the original. None of the buyers could go to the police because they were guilty of buying goods they believed to be stolen. By returning the original the thieves ensured that they would get only a light punishment if they were caught.

The Murderer

Brown confessed to Father Smith in the confessional. Father Smith was prevented from telling the police by the seal of the confessional.

The Music Stopped Again

He was an insect sitting on a chair seat during a game of musical chairs.

The Newspaper

She slid the sheet of newspaper under a door. The boys stood on either side of the door but on the same piece of paper.

Not a Hair

Lyndsey had accepted the role of a Deltan in a "Star Trek" movie. Deltan women are noted for shaving their heads.

On Time

The man is having an affair. Once he has phoned his mistress, he calls the speaking clock so that if his wife should later press the redial button she will not find out anything he does not want her to know.

One Croaked!

The frogs fell into a large tank of cream. One swam around for a while but then gave up and drowned. The other kept swimming until his movements turned the cream into knobs of butter, on which he safely floated.

Order Delayed

The man had ordered a Seven-Up. The hotel receptionist had misunderstood the order for the soda to mean a wake-up call for 7 a.m.

Penniless

The author's wife was the lady admirer. She had recently received a small legacy and did not want to offend him by offering him money directly.

Personality Plus

The man was ambidextrous. He gave two writing samples under different names—one written with his right hand and one with his left. The agency gave him two completely different personality profiles.

The Plate of Mushrooms

He was to be executed. The mushrooms were his last meal.

Poison Pen

The sheet of paper on which the letter had been written had been taken from a writing pad. On the previous sheet, the culprit had written his address. This caused a slight impression on the sheet below. The address became visible when the policeman gently shaded the sheet with pencil.

Poisoned

The man was separated from his wife but wanted to be reconciled. His nephew, and heir, suggested showing how distraught he was at the loss of his wife by staging a suicide attempt and taking an overdose. The nephew agreed to take the man's last, farewell letter to his wife so that she would rush round and save the man. Instead of doing so, the callous nephew stuck a stamp on it and posted it. By the time the wife reached her husband, he was dead.

Price Tag

The practice originated to ensure that the clerk had to open the till and give change for each transaction, thus recording the sale and preventing him from pocketing the bills.

Rich Man, Poor Man

He works at the mint. He makes many millions of dollars a year but draws a modest salary.

A Riddle

For the music they played,
Each band member was paid.

Scout's Honor

She covered the stains with a bandage strip. Nobody would remove it to check whether he had a cut.

Seaside Idea

As he watched his children skimming stones on the water he got the idea for the famous bouncing bombs used by the "Dam Busters" in their raid against German dams. The bombs bounced along the surface of the lakes before hitting the dams and flooding large industrial areas.

Self-Addressed Envelope

The man lives in a remote spot ten miles from the bar in the nearest village. If the postman calls on him to deliver any mail, then the man can get a lift from the postman into the village. Otherwise he has to pay for a taxi. He secretly sends himself a letter every day to get the postman to call. The postman does not deliver on Sunday, so there is no need for a letter to be posted on Saturday.

Silence Is Golden

The talk, given by a doctor, was on the subject of breast-feeding. It was given to a group of nursing mothers all of whom had their babies with them. They agreed that applause would wake and scare the babies, so they waved their hands in the air instead.

The Single Flower

She opened the window and a bee flew into the room. It settled on the one true flower.

Sleeping on the Job

The man was Clark Gable, the screen idol, who took off his shirt in a movie in which he was about to go to bed. He was not wearing an undershirt. So great was his influence that men stopped wearing undershirts and factories making them had to close down. In a later movie, he wore an undershirt and restored it to fashion.

Snow Joy

There is a rule in that county that up to six "snow days" may be lost from the school calendar because of bad weather. If the bad weather extends past six days, then each additional day lost must be made up by the school working an extra day—which is taken from the summer vacation. The children were upset that they would now lose precious holidays in the summer.

Souper

Her contact lens had fallen into the soup and she wanted to retrieve it.

Soviet Pictures

In a group of ten Soviet officials photographed sitting around a table there were eleven pairs of feet underneath the table.

The Stranger in the Bar

He said, "I am the taxi driver who has been driving you from bar to bar!"

The Stranger in the Hotel

She reasoned that if it had really been his room he would not have knocked at the door but used his key. (She was on a corridor of single rooms, so it was unlikely he was sharing.) In fact, he knocked in order to check whether anyone was in before using a pass key to enter and burgle rooms.

The String and the Cloth

His kite had snagged across some electricity power lines. It was raining. He had been electrocuted. The cloth and string were the remains of the kite.

The Task

This is a true story that happened some years ago in New York during a power outage. A telephone exchange in a large apartment building was working on an independent power supply. Many people wanted to phone out, to reassure friends and relatives. They were helped in this by a blind man, who could do a much better job of dialing numbers in the pitch dark than any of them could.

These Puzzles

Each puzzle contains a question. The pronoun of the question determines the category. All the "what" questions are in the Aquamarine section, the "how" questions are in the Orange section (together with one "who" question) and the "why" questions are in the Yellow section. (The first vowels of the pronouns are A, O and Y.)

Truckload

It was a long bridge and the weight of gasoline used in reaching the center of the bridge exceeds the weight of the flock of starlings. The truck still weighs no more than 10 tons.

Unknown Character

He called the local sheriff, who had never heard of him. He used this as proof of his good character.

The Unlucky Trip

The torch was the Olympic Torch, which the hurrying man was carrying to the opening of the Olympic Games.

Unpublished

The manuscript was for the book of the famous play *The Mousetrap* by Agatha Christie. She had requested that for as long as it ran as a play in London's West End, it should not be published as a novel (for fear of giving away the play's secret). Little could she have foreseen that the play would set a world record for the longest run of over 40 years' continuous performances.

Unseen

A woman! The man was Mihailo Tolotos, who was taken from his mother at birth and who spent all his life in the Greek monastery of Athos, where no females were allowed.

Unspoken Understanding

He gives the cashier four quarters, from which the cashier correctly deduces that the man wants two 40-cent tokens.

The Unwanted Gift

The King was the King of Siam and the gift was a white elephant. The story goes that the King gave the gift of a rare white elephant to those with whom he was displeased and wished to ruin. The elephant was very expensive to keep but was sacred and could not be used for work. Also as a royal gift, it could not be disposed of. This is the source of the expression "a white elephant."

Upstairs, Downstairs

It is the First Class restaurant on a luxury ocean liner. Upstairs is out on deck. If it rains the entire company transfers downstairs and takes up where it left off.

What a Bore!

She has a cellular phone in her pocket. Discreetly, she presses a button on it that causes it to give a test ring. She pretends that she has been awaiting an important call that she must take.

What a Jump!

It was a ski jump.

What a Relief!

It was to collect penicillin, the new wonder drug. It was in very short supply, but American soldiers were given it to protect them against various diseases. The easiest way for French doctors to get hold of penicillin was to extract it from the urine of the GIs.

Where in the World?

On a pack of playing cards. The original designs for the Kings, Queens and Jacks are based on these characters.

Wino

His host had sneezed and the guest felt that his dessert had been contaminated. He did not want to eat it, nor did he want to blame his host, so he deliberately knocked the salt into the dessert. He made it look like an accident.

The Wounded Soldier

The surgeon had run out of life-saving adrenaline. He knew that the soldier was badly wounded and hoped to provoke a rush of natural adrenaline through the soldier's reaction to his false accusation.

The Yacht Incident

All of the people on the yacht went swimming. No one put a rope ladder over the side. They were unable to get back on board again.

WALLY Test I Answers

Here are the answers to the first WALLY test—get ready to kick yourself!

1. Eight days. Each day he takes out one ear of corn and two squirrel ears!

2. The first triangle is larger—one with sides measuring 200, 300 and 400 cm. The triangle with sides measuring 300, 400 and 700 cm has an area of zero!

3. Halfway—after that, it is running out of the wood.

4. In total darkness none of them could see a thing.

5. Mount Everest.

6. On the head.

7. The President would remain President.

8. No candles burn longer—all candles burn shorter.

9. He had one large haystack.

10. Short.

11. A pound of feathers weighs more than a pound of gold. Gold is measured in Troy pounds, which weigh less than the regular Avoirdupois pounds in which items such as feathers would be weighed.

12. A bed.

Rate your score on the following scale:

Number Correct	Rating
12 to 14	WALLY Whiz
8 to 11	Smart Alec
4 to 7	WALLY
0 to 3	Ultra-WALLY

WALLY Test II Answers

More answers—more groans! Or maybe you did better on this second test.

1. 1 and 17.
2. Bread.
3. Sixes.
4. In England, it is not usual to bury people who are still alive.
5. One—after that, his stomach is not empty.
6. The Unfinished Symphony was written by Schubert.
7. Wrongly.
8. A hole.
9. You would be losing 45 cents. I gave you 30 cents in exchange for the three quarters.
10. 12.

Rate your score on the following scale:

Number Correct	Rating
8 to 10	WALLY Whiz
6 to 7	Smart Alec
3 to 5	WALLY
0 to 2	Ultra-WALLY

About the Authors

PAUL SLOANE was born in Scotland and grew up near Blackpool in the north of England. He studied engineering at Trinity Hall, Cambridge, and graduated with a first-class honors degree. While at Cambridge he met his wife, Ann, who is a teacher. They live in Camberley, England, with their three daughters.

Most of Paul Sloane's career has been in the computer industry and he is currently the European vice-president for a software company. He has always been an avid collector and creator of puzzles. His first book, *Lateral Thinking Puzzlers*, was published by Sterling in 1991. Paul Sloane has given speeches and radio talks on the topic of change management and lateral thinking.

DES MACHALE was born in County Mayo, Ireland, and is Associate Professor of Mathematics at University College in Cork. He was educated at University College, Galway, and the University of Keele in England. He and his wife, Anne, have five children.

The author of over thirty books, mostly of humor but also one on giving up smoking, Des MacHale has many interests, including puzzles, geology, writing, broadcasting, films, photography, numismatics and, of course, mathematics. He is currently working on several new projects.

This is the fifth book co-authored by Paul Sloane and Des MacHale, following the success of their other lateral thinking puzzle books, also published by Sterling.

Index

Page key: puzzle, *clue*, **solution**